MAKE it WORK!

FLIGHT

Andrew Haslam

written by
Jack Challoner

Photography
Jon Barnes

World Book

in association with
TWO-CAN

MAKE it WORK!
Other titles

World Book, Inc., 233 N. Michigan Ave.
Suite 2000, Chicago, IL 60601
in association with Two-Can Publishing

2006 printing
Copyright © Two-Can Publishing, 1998
Design © Andrew Haslam

For information about other World Book publications, visit our Web site <u>http://www.worldbook.com</u> or call 1-800-WORLDBK (967-5325). For information about sales to schools and libraries call 1-800-975-3250 (United States); 1-800-837-5365 (Canada).

Library of Congress Cataloging-in-Publication data
Haslam, Andrew
    Flight / Andrew Haslam; written by Jack Challoner: photography by John Barnes.
    Previously published: Flight/written by Jack Challoner, New York: Thomson Learning, 1995
Includes index.
    Summary: Introduces basic facts about the properties of flight with instructions for related experiments and projects.
    ISBN 0-7166-4714-1 (hc) — ISBN 0-7166-4715-X (sc)
    1. Flight—Experiments—Juvenile literature. 2. Aerodynamics—Experiments— Juvenile literature. 3. Aeronautics—Juvenile literature. [1. Flight—Experiments. 2. Aerodynamics—Experiments. 3. Experiments.] I. Challoner, Jack. II. Barnes, Jon, ill. III. Challoner, Jack. Flight IV. Title V Series:
TL547.H37 1998
629.132'3'0078-dc21   98-13422

Printed in China

5 6 7 8 9 10 09 08 07 06

Editor: Kate Asser
Editor: Dr Kathryn Senior
Series concept and original design: Andrew Haslam and Wendy Baker
Designer: Peter Claymore
U. S. Editor: Melissa Tucker, World Book Publishing
Thanks also to: Cordel Eliss, Rachel and Jonathon Bee, and everyone at Plough Studios

Contents

Words marked in **bold** in the
text are explained in the glossary.

Today, there are many different flying machines. There are airplanes, gliders, hot-air balloons, airships, and even rockets that fly beyond the **atmosphere**. But how did we learn to fly? And how does a heavy airplane stay in the air?

Building different aircraft

Airplanes are designed for different uses. Fighter jets must be fast and easy to maneuver, and airplanes that carry passengers need to be safe and comfortable. The materials used to build airplanes have different properties, too. Most parts need to be strong and light, while some parts need to bend, and others have to withstand intense heat.

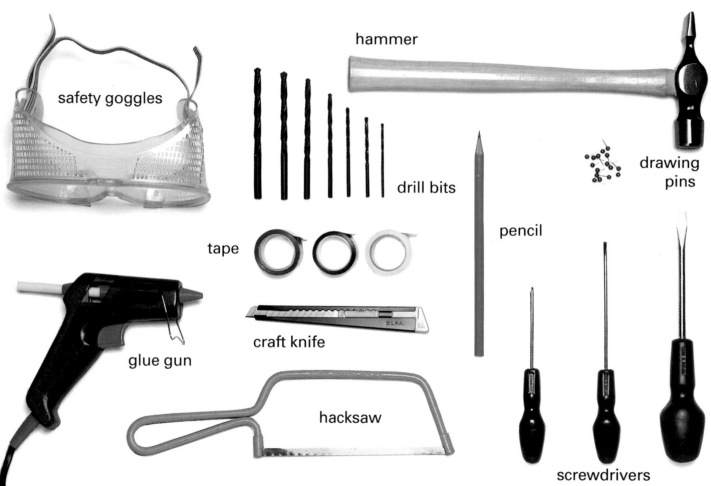

safety goggles

hammer

drill bits

drawing pins

pencil

tape

craft knife

glue gun

hacksaw

screwdrivers

Four **forces** act·on any flying object. **Gravity** pulls an aircraft down toward the earth. Wings produce **lift**, which works upward against gravity as the aircraft moves in the air. A third force, **thrust**, pushes an aircraft forward, and **drag**, or **air resistance**, slows it down. To get an object airborne, lift and thrust have to overcome gravity and drag.

MAKE it WORK!

You don't need to build airplanes that fly at **supersonic** speeds to learn more about flight. The projects in this book show you how to make different types of flying models and reveal the secrets of how they stay in the air. Many of the projects concentrate on airplanes, but other things fly, too. By making a boomerang, an arrow, a flying disk, a rotor, and even a powerful rocket, you will see that some things stay in the air more easily than others.

You will need

For each project you will find a list of the things you need to make the model. Most materials can be found around the home. Cardboard, paper clips, string, and thread spools are often needed. You may also need to buy a few things. Balsa wood is very useful for making flying models, as it is both strong and light. You also will need a few basic tools. Some of the equipment shown below will come in handy for many of the projects.

Drilling

For some of the projects in this book, you will need to drill holes. Use a pointed awl to start the holes and finish them with a hand drill. This stops the drill bit from sliding around. Make sure that the bit is the correct size.

Joining

A glue stick used with a glue gun is an easy way to join parts of your model together. Let the glue dry before performing test flights.

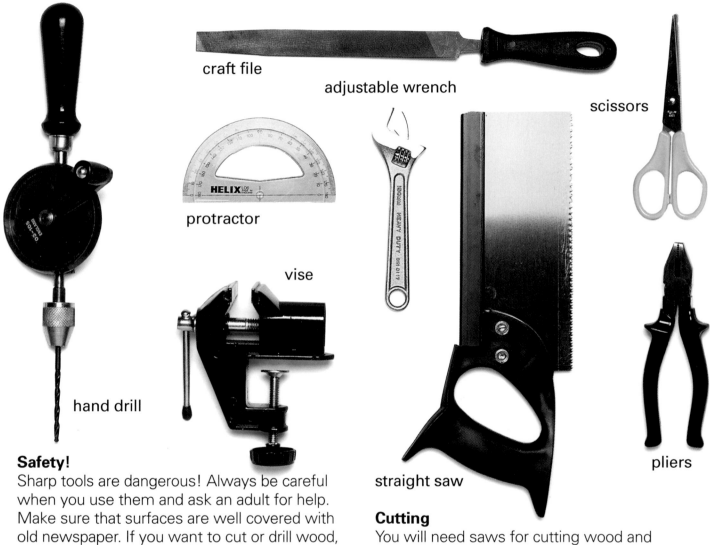

craft file

adjustable wrench

scissors

protractor

vise

hand drill

straight saw

pliers

Safety!

Sharp tools are dangerous! Always be careful when you use them and ask an adult for help. Make sure that surfaces are well covered with old newspaper. If you want to cut or drill wood, use a small table vise to hold the pieces firmly so that they do not slip.

Planning

Always plan projects before you start. Read the instructions carefully, and take a close look at the photographs.

Cutting

You will need saws for cutting wood and scissors for cutting cardboard and paper. A craft knife is useful, too. It is always better to ask an adult to cut with a saw or knife for you as they have sharp blades. Measure each part accurately before cutting and always cut away from your body. Smooth over rough edges of wood or polystyrene with sandpaper or a file.

Birds in Flight

Many years ago, scientists used photographs of birds in flight to help them understand how birds fly. They found that it was the movement and shape of the birds' wings that made flight possible. The feathers at the wing tips produce thrust, pushing the bird through the air. The shape of the wings causes lift as air moves over them.

1 Use a compass to draw two circles, each with a **radius** of 5 inches. Draw one circle on corrugated cardboard and the other on paper.

2 Mark the centers of the circles and then cut the circles out carefully.

3 Using a protractor, mark the outlines of 10 equally spaced slits. They should be 36° apart and measure 1¼ x ¼ inches on the paper circle. Your circle should look like the one below. Do the same for the cardboard circle.

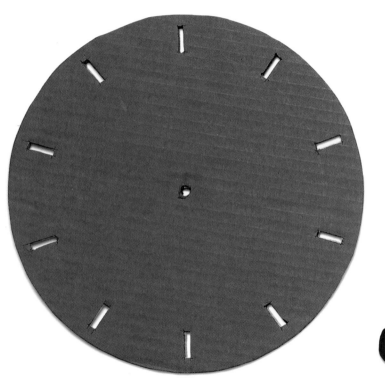

MAKE it WORK!
A spinning disk called a **phenakistoscope** causes a series of drawings to appear as a moving picture. You can use a phenakistoscope to study how birds move their wings in flight.

You will need
a pen	modeling clay
paper	paper glue
scissors	a craft knife
a compass	a large mirror
a protractor	a wooden dowel
corrugated cardboard	old newspapers

4 Put a thick layer of old newspaper over your table or desktop to protect it. Ask an adult to help you cut out the slits in both circles using a craft knife.

5 Set the cardboard circle to one side. Copy the 10 bird drawings shown, above right, as accurately as you can onto the paper circle, beneath each slit.

6 Line up the slits in both circles so that you can see through them. Glue the paper circle to the cardboard circle, plain side down.

7 Make a hole through the center of both circles and push the dowel through. Secure the dowel with a lump of modeling clay.

8 Stand the mirror up and sit in front of it. Hold your phenakistoscope in front of the mirror, as shown. Look through the slits from behind and turn the dowel in your fingers. You should be able to see a bird in flight.

For hundreds of years people tried to copy the motion of flying birds. They attached wings to themselves and flapped as hard as they could. But all their attempts failed. Humans would need to have much stronger muscles and much lighter bodies to be able to fly like birds.

Just as a spinning top will not topple as long as it stays spinning, so the spin of a boomerang or a flying disk gives it **stability** in the air. When you throw a flying disk, it is launched with its front edge higher than its back edge. This produces lift, which helps it to stay in the air longer. A boomerang's spin and curved shape cause it to change direction as it flies.

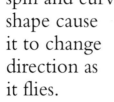

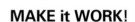

MAKE it WORK!
See if you can find the best way to launch your own flying disk and boomerang.

To make a flying disk you will need
an aluminum pie pan   modeling clay

1 Press three small balls of modeling clay onto the outside edge of the pan at equal distances apart.

2 Launch your disk with one hand, as shown above. As you release it, flick your wrist forward to make the disk spin. Does it fly better with a fast or slow spin?

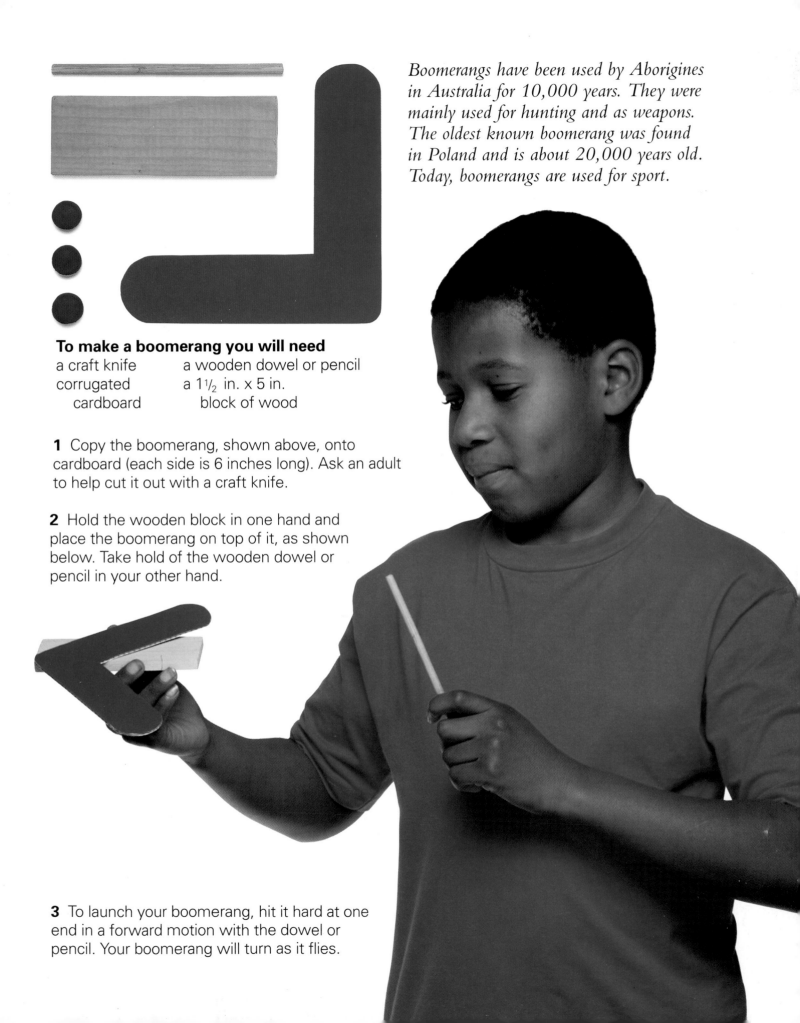

Boomerangs have been used by Aborigines in Australia for 10,000 years. They were mainly used for hunting and as weapons. The oldest known boomerang was found in Poland and is about 20,000 years old. Today, boomerangs are used for sport.

To make a boomerang you will need

a craft knife
corrugated
   cardboard

a wooden dowel or pencil
a 1½ in. x 5 in.
   block of wood

1 Copy the boomerang, shown above, onto cardboard (each side is 6 inches long). Ask an adult to help cut it out with a craft knife.

2 Hold the wooden block in one hand and place the boomerang on top of it, as shown below. Take hold of the wooden dowel or pencil in your other hand.

3 To launch your boomerang, hit it hard at one end in a forward motion with the dowel or pencil. Your boomerang will turn as it flies.

10 Bows and Arrows

The bow and arrow has been used for over 30,000 years as a fast and accurate hunting weapon. The vanes at the end of an arrow help it to fly straight. As soon as an arrow is released from a bow, it is slowed by air resistance. The faster an arrow moves, the farther it travels before hitting the ground. Because arrows are long and straight, drag is reduced.

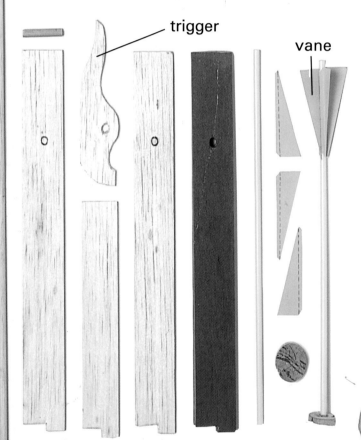

trigger

vane

MAKE it WORK!

This crossbow uses **energy** from muscles in the archer's arm to make arrows fly. As the bowstring is pulled back, energy from muscles in the arm transfers to the **strained** bow. This stored energy makes the arrow shoot forward when the string is released. Make your own crossbow and find out how vanes affect the accuracy of arrows.

You will need

a cork	glue
a saw	a hand drill
string	balsa wood
poster board	a craft knife
wooden dowel	a sewing needle
a drinking straw	

1 Carefully cut a wooden dowel about 30 in. long. Tie 3 ft. of string to the dowel at both ends, as shown left, to make a bow.

2 To make the handle, cut two pieces of balsa wood, 2 in. x 12 in. and 1½ in. x 7 in. Make a notch in one end of each piece, as shown left. Cut out another piece 5 in. long for the trigger.

3 Drill holes through the handle pieces and trigger. Make them big enough to allow a short wooden dowel to fit through.

4 Line up the notched ends of the balsa wood pieces. Glue them together with the 7-in. piece in the middle and let dry.

5 Slip the trigger in between the long pieces of balsa wood. Line up the holes and put in the dowel.

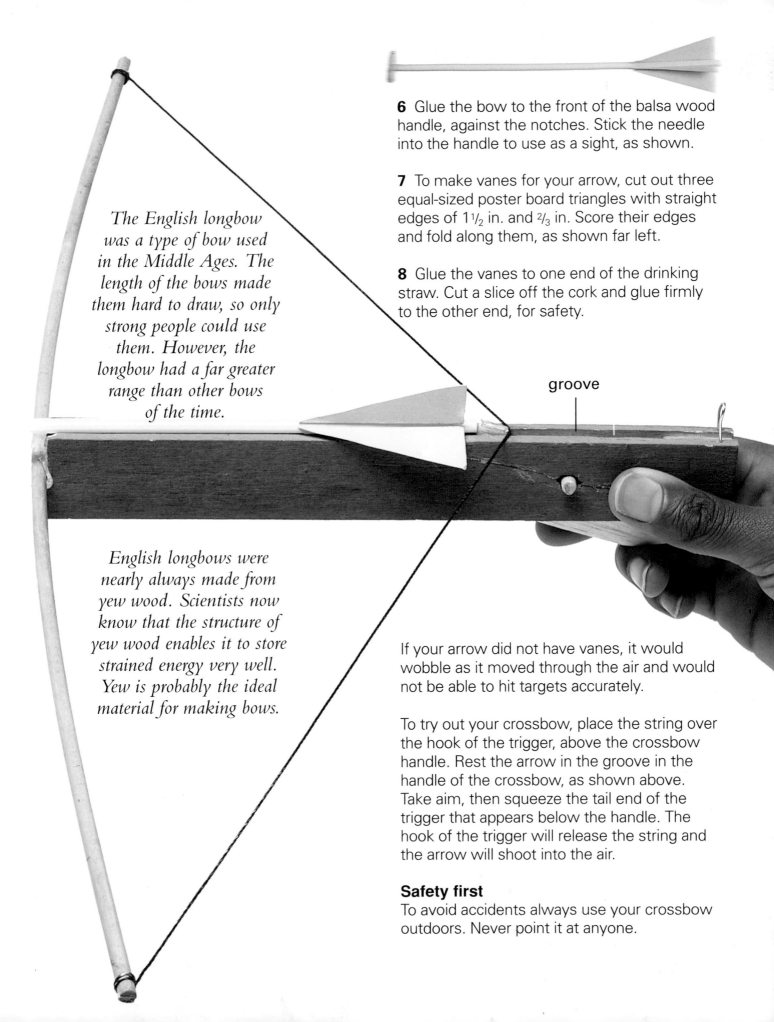

The English longbow was a type of bow used in the Middle Ages. The length of the bows made them hard to draw, so only strong people could use them. However, the longbow had a far greater range than other bows of the time.

English longbows were nearly always made from yew wood. Scientists now know that the structure of yew wood enables it to store strained energy very well. Yew is probably the ideal material for making bows.

6 Glue the bow to the front of the balsa wood handle, against the notches. Stick the needle into the handle to use as a sight, as shown.

7 To make vanes for your arrow, cut out three equal-sized poster board triangles with straight edges of 1½ in. and ⅔ in. Score their edges and fold along them, as shown far left.

8 Glue the vanes to one end of the drinking straw. Cut a slice off the cork and glue firmly to the other end, for safety.

groove

If your arrow did not have vanes, it would wobble as it moved through the air and would not be able to hit targets accurately.

To try out your crossbow, place the string over the hook of the trigger, above the crossbow handle. Rest the arrow in the groove in the handle of the crossbow, as shown above. Take aim, then squeeze the tail end of the trigger that appears below the handle. The hook of the trigger will release the string and the arrow will shoot into the air.

Safety first
To avoid accidents always use your crossbow outdoors. Never point it at anyone.

12 Cannons

To make large objects fly through the air we need a force large enough to overcome the pull of gravity. Centuries ago, people found that exploding gunpowder in a cannon provided the force to lift a cannonball into the air and push it forward. However, once a cannonball has been expelled, gravity and air resistance slow the ball down, causing it to fall to the ground.

You will need
glue
a protractor
thumb tacks
poster board
a long rubber band
a thin wooden dowel
a thick wooden dowel
corrugated cardboard
a clay flowerpot
colored tape and carpet tape
two cardboard tubes of different widths
a ping-pong ball to fit inside the larger tube

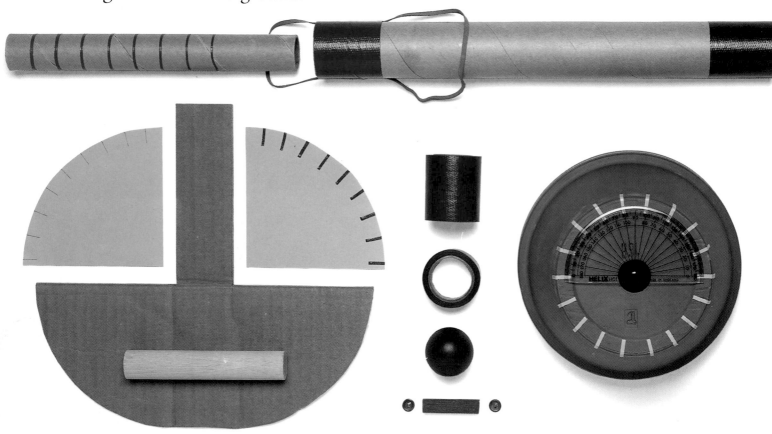

MAKE it WORK!
This homemade cannon uses the force from a stretched rubber band to fire cannonballs. The ball is forced upward and forward through the air, traveling in a curved path called a **trajectory**. But gravity is always acting on the ball, pulling it downward toward the earth. You can use your cannon to investigate trajectories of cannonballs.

1 For the turret, cut corrugated cardboard and poster board into the shapes shown above left. The segments have a radius of 6 in. Using the protractor, mark the thin cardboard pieces with strips of tape every 10°.

2 Fold the corrugated cardboard and glue the thin poster board to the sides, as shown right. Join the sides of turret at the top, using a small piece of dowel and thumb tacks.

3 Cut a length of thick dowel long enough to stand slightly higher than the flowerpot. Turn the flowerpot upside down and put the dowel through the hole.

4 Using the protractor, mark around the top of the flowerpot every 20°. Stick strips of brightly colored tape over the marks, as shown below. Glue the base of the turret to the dowel.

5 Take the narrow cardboard tube and mark every inch along the outside. Place it inside the wider tube (the barrel of the cannon).

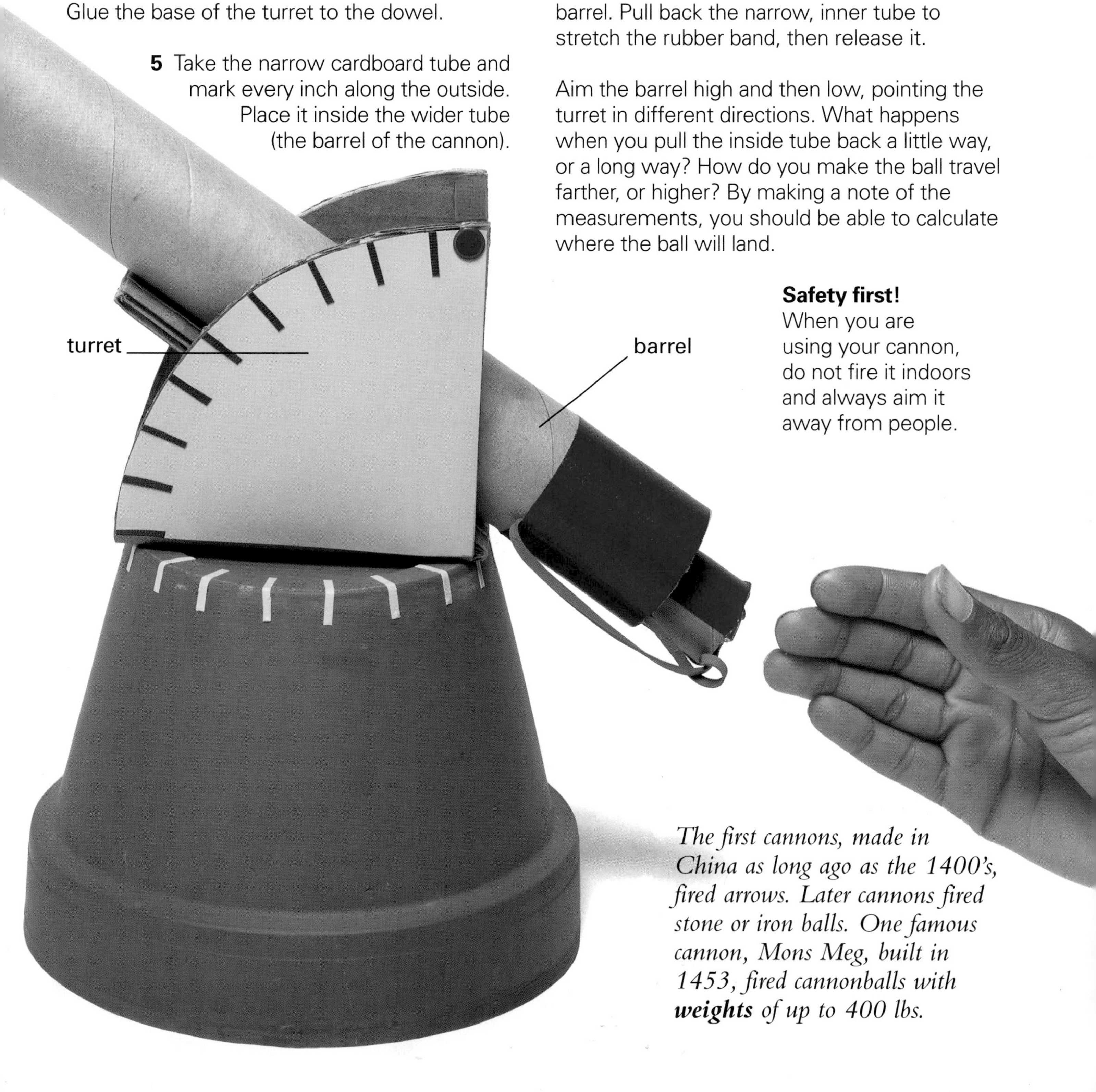

6 Using carpet tape, attach the rubber band to the bottom end of the barrel and to the bottom end of the narrow tube, as shown.

7 Glue the barrel of the cannon to the movable flap inside the turret.

8 To fire the cannon, place the ball inside the barrel. Pull back the narrow, inner tube to stretch the rubber band, then release it.

Aim the barrel high and then low, pointing the turret in different directions. What happens when you pull the inside tube back a little way, or a long way? How do you make the ball travel farther, or higher? By making a note of the measurements, you should be able to calculate where the ball will land.

turret

barrel

Safety first!
When you are using your cannon, do not fire it indoors and always aim it away from people.

*The first cannons, made in China as long ago as the 1400's, fired arrows. Later cannons fired stone or iron balls. One famous cannon, Mons Meg, built in 1453, fired cannonballs with **weights** of up to 400 lbs.*

Kites were invented in China nearly 3,000 years ago. They fly because they get lift from the wind. The stronger the wind, the greater the force pushing the kite into the air. To keep flying, the kite must be held at an angle against the wind (called the angle of attack), just as a sail must face into the wind to move a sailboat. Control lines are used to keep the kite at the correct angle to the wind.

1 Cut the nylon or polyethylene into a kite shape, 30 in. long and 28 in. across. Using an awl, make two holes in the kite, one 1 in. below the top point, the other 5 in. below. Make a hole about 1 in. in from each side point.

2 Being careful of your fingers, make two pairs of holes at right angles to each other through one piece of tubing. Push the tubing halfway into the hole at the top of the kite.

3 Pass the rigid dowel through the plastic tubing, as in **a** below. Push the flexible dowel through the other holes in the tubing, as in **b**.

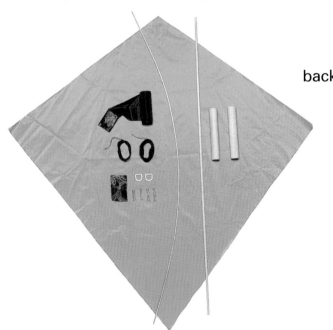

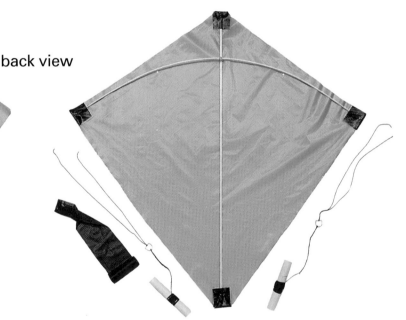

back view

MAKE it WORK!

You can make your own kite and experiment with the forces that keep it in the air. Use the lines to control the kite and see how long you can keep it flying!

You will need

an awl	two metal rings
nylon cord	a craft knife
a long ribbon	carpet tape
five short pieces of plastic tubing	scissors
3 sq. ft. of polyethylene or nylon	ruler
thick, rigid dowel about 30 in. long	
thin, flexible dowel about 35 in. long	
two lengths of broom handle about 6 in. long	

4 Make holes in the other pieces of tubing. Push three of the pieces into holes at the sides and top of the kite. Stick the rigid dowel into the top and bottom tubes, and the flexible dowel into the side tubes. Fold the corners over the tubes and tape securely.

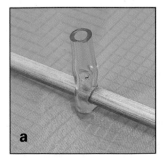

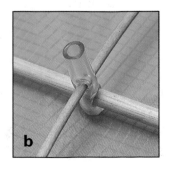

To make your kite fly, stand with your back to the wind. Then run backward, pulling the kite to get it airborne.

To make the kite turn to the right, pull on the right handle. To make it fly straight again, pull on the left handle.

To make the kite turn to the left, pull on the left handle. To straighten the kite out, pull with your right hand.

back view

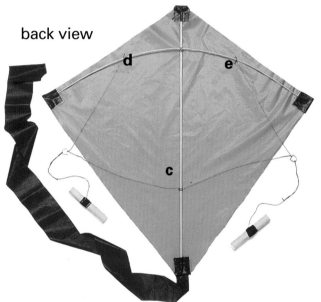

front view

5 Make three holes at points **c**, **d**, and **e**. Tie the middle of a 30 in. length of cord around the rigid dowel at **c**. Push both ends through hole **c** to the front of the kite. Turn the kite onto its front. Thread each end of the cord through a metal ring. Push the ends through to the back again, one at **d** and one at **e**, tying each to the flexible dowel.

6 Cut 26 ft. of cord in half. Tape one end of each half to a broom handle and tie the other to the rings. Wind the cord around the handles. Tape the tail ribbon onto the kite, as shown.

About 1,000 years ago, the Chinese used kites to lift soldiers into the sky to survey battlefields.

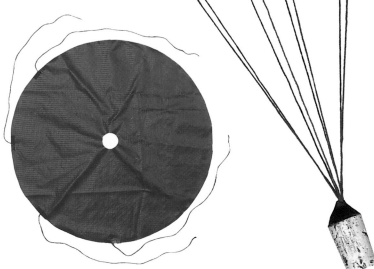

The force of air resistance acts on anything moving through the air. Without air resistance, or drag, objects would fall even faster than they do. The larger the object, the greater its air resistance. Parachutes use a large canopy to increase air resistance. This gives a slow fall and a soft landing.

MAKE it WORK!

Can you find the best parachute design? Also, make a simple spinner and watch its wings spin as air resistance pushes against them.

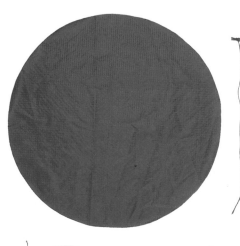

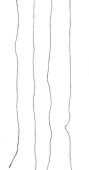

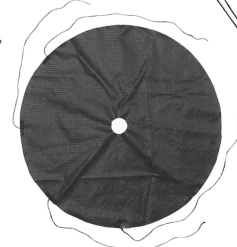

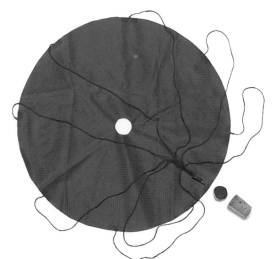

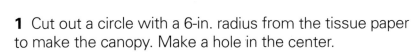

To make a parachute you will need

modeling clay	tape	scissors
tissue paper	a cork	
sewing thread	a small nail	

1 Cut out a circle with a 6-in. radius from the tissue paper to make the canopy. Make a hole in the center.

2 Cut eight 12-in. pieces of sewing thread. Tape them at equal distances around the canopy edge, as shown above.

3 Tape the other ends of the threads to the nail and push the nail into the cork. Use modeling clay to secure the nail.

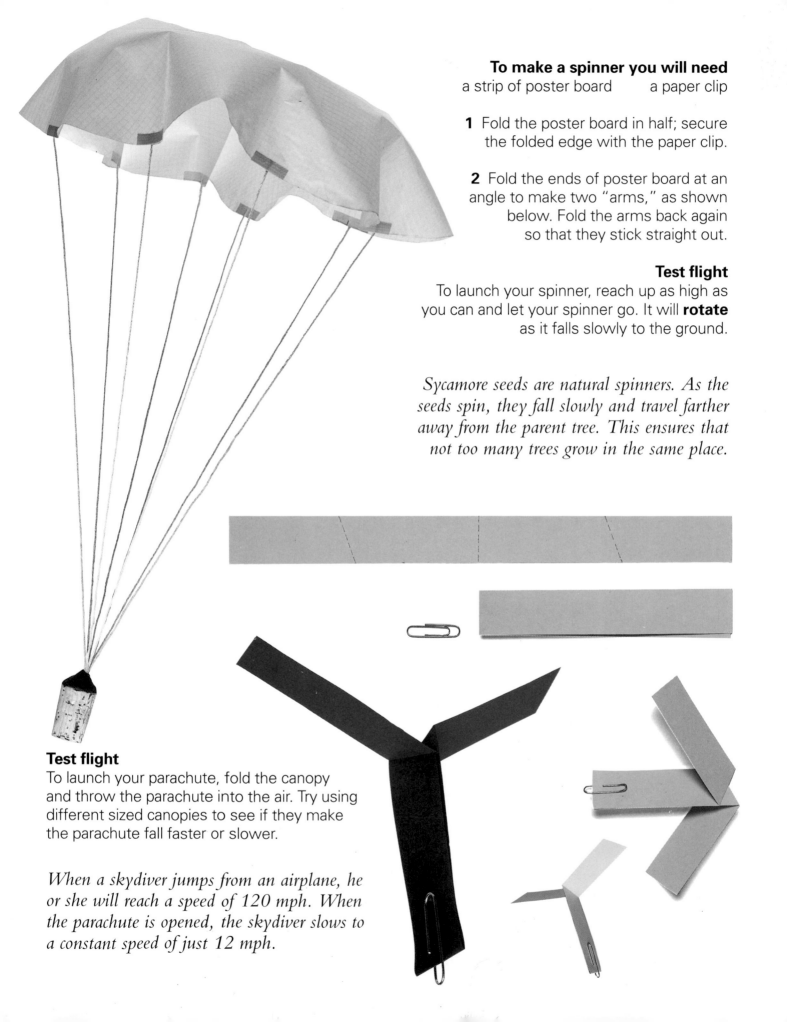

To make a spinner you will need

a strip of poster board   a paper clip

1 Fold the poster board in half; secure the folded edge with the paper clip.

2 Fold the ends of poster board at an angle to make two "arms," as shown below. Fold the arms back again so that they stick straight out.

Test flight

To launch your spinner, reach up as high as you can and let your spinner go. It will **rotate** as it falls slowly to the ground.

Sycamore seeds are natural spinners. As the seeds spin, they fall slowly and travel farther away from the parent tree. This ensures that not too many trees grow in the same place.

Test flight

To launch your parachute, fold the canopy and throw the parachute into the air. Try using different sized canopies to see if they make the parachute fall faster or slower.

When a skydiver jumps from an airplane, he or she will reach a speed of 120 mph. When the parachute is opened, the skydiver slows to a constant speed of just 12 mph.

Hot air is less **dense** than cold air. Hot air therefore rises through cold air and floats on it, just as oil floats on water. A balloon filled with hot air is less dense than cold air, so the whole balloon rises. Hot air can lift large balloons to great heights.

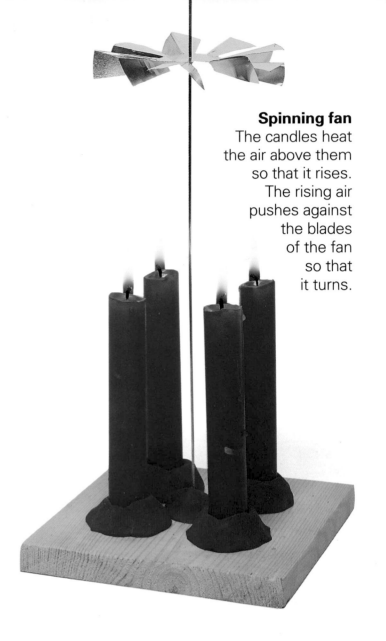

Spinning fan
The candles heat the air above them so that it rises. The rising air pushes against the blades of the fan so that it turns.

MAKE it WORK!
These experiments prove that hot air rises.
Be careful! Never leave lit candles unattended.

For the spinning fan you will need
four candles	stiff wire
a wooden block	modeling clay
an aluminum pie pan	a small bead

1 Fix the candles and the wire onto the block with clay, as shown. Thread and tape the bead onto the wire 6 in. above the candles.

2 Cut blades from the pan and angle them, as shown. Thread the "fan" onto the wire so that it sits on the bead. Ask an adult to light the candles.

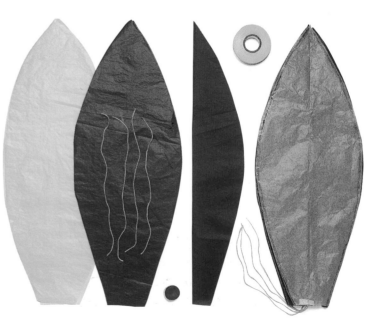

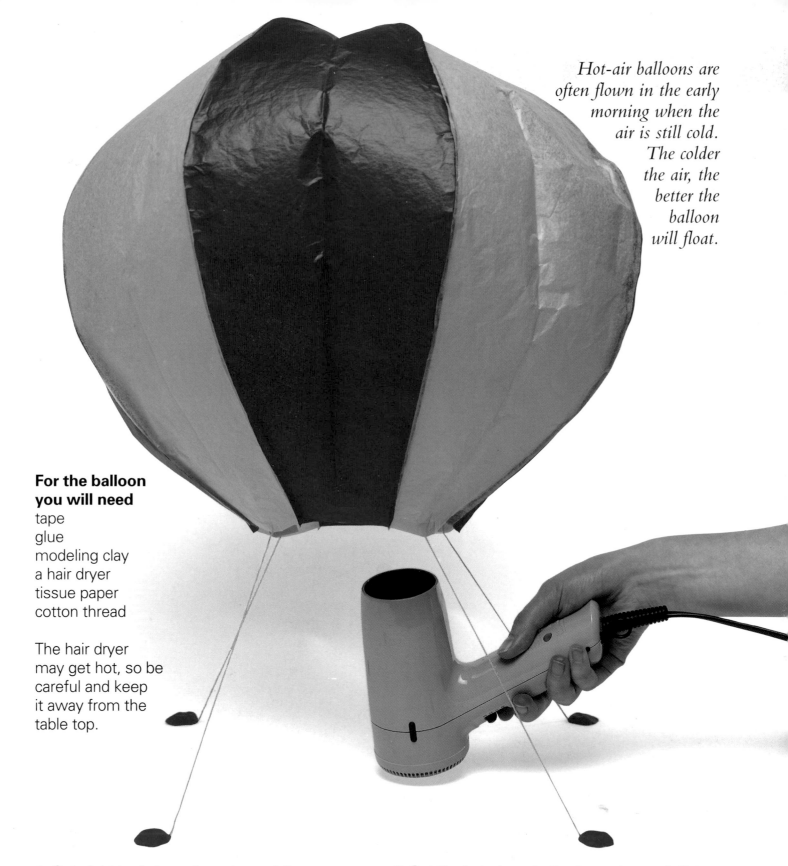

Hot-air balloons are often flown in the early morning when the air is still cold. The colder the air, the better the balloon will float.

For the balloon you will need
tape
glue
modeling clay
a hair dryer
tissue paper
cotton thread

The hair dryer may get hot, so be careful and keep it away from the table top.

1 Cut eight leaf-shaped sections of tissue paper, as shown left. Fold them in half and glue the edges together to make the balloon. Tape four threads to the bottom of the balloon. Fix the loose ends to a table with clay.

2 Set the hair dryer to the lowest speed. Point the nozzle upward into the hole in the base of the balloon and turn the power on. The balloon will fill with hot air and will pull the threads tight, as shown above.

Airships are filled with a gas called helium. Helium floats in air because, like hot air, it is lighter than cold air. Helium gives enough lift to an airship to allow it to carry many passengers or cargo. Large propellers, driven by an engine, provide the thrust that pushes an airship forward through the air. A tail fin gives the airship stability when it is in flight.

MAKE it WORK!
You can make an airship with helium-filled party balloons. You must tether your airship to the ground to keep it from floating away.

You will need

tape	glue
scissors	string
poster board	modeling clay
four helium-filled balloons	

1 Cut a tail fin, tailplanes, and cabin from poster board, as shown above. The cabin is 7 in. long.

2 Cut eight pieces of string into equal lengths. Weight each string with a piece of modeling clay and tape to either side of the balloons to balance your airship, as shown above right.

3 Make your airship by gluing the balloons together. Tether it to the ground with string.

4 Fold up the poster board for the cabin and secure it with tape. Hang the cabin from the middle balloons with tape and string, as shown.

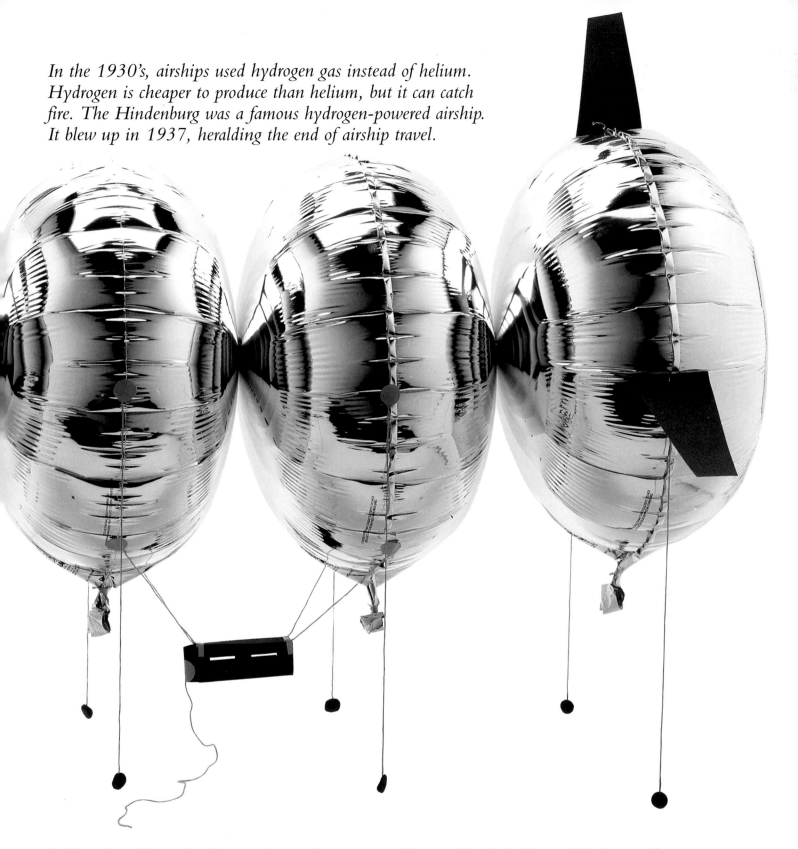

In the 1930's, airships used hydrogen gas instead of helium. Hydrogen is cheaper to produce than helium, but it can catch fire. The Hindenburg was a famous hydrogen-powered airship. It blew up in 1937, heralding the end of airship travel.

5 Glue the tail fin and tailplane pieces of poster board to the airship tail, as shown.

6 Add or take away modeling clay from the ends of the strings hanging from each balloon until your airship hangs upright in the air.

Eventually, the helium will leak out of your airship. If it begins to come down, remove some clay from the strings to make it lighter. Real airships contain bags called ballonets inside the helium. To bring the airship down, the ballonets are filled with air, which is heavier than helium.

22 Gliders

Gliders have no source of **power**. As soon as they are launched, they begin to fall back toward the ground. To keep flying, a glider pilot must find rising currents of warm air, called thermals, which lift the glider. When flying, the pilot controls the glider using pedals connected to the rudder.

1 Cut a 16-in. length of dowel for the fuselage and a 4-in. length for the launcher.

2 To make the wings, cut out a piece of cardboard 2 in. x 12 in. Cut out a tailplane 2 in. x 8 in. at the widest point. Cut a tail fin 3 in. high and a rudder 2¾ in. high.

3 Glue a 2-in. strip of balsa wood to the center of the wings. Glue the strip to the fuselage, so the wings are about 4 in. from the nose.

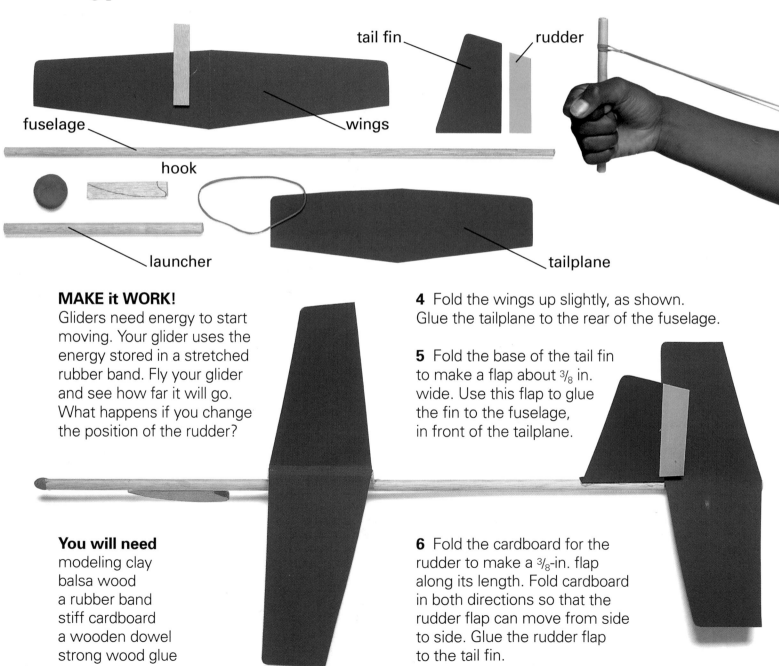

tail fin

rudder

wings

fuselage

hook

launcher

tailplane

MAKE it WORK!

Gliders need energy to start moving. Your glider uses the energy stored in a stretched rubber band. Fly your glider and see how far it will go. What happens if you change the position of the rudder?

You will need

modeling clay
balsa wood
a rubber band
stiff cardboard
a wooden dowel
strong wood glue

4 Fold the wings up slightly, as shown. Glue the tailplane to the rear of the fuselage.

5 Fold the base of the tail fin to make a flap about ⅜ in. wide. Use this flap to glue the fin to the fuselage, in front of the tailplane.

6 Fold the cardboard for the rudder to make a ⅜-in. flap along its length. Fold cardboard in both directions so that the rudder flap can move from side to side. Glue the rudder flap to the tail fin.

7 Rest your glider on your finger just under the wings. It will tip toward the tailplane. To make the glider balance, add modeling clay to the glider's nose.

8 Cut out a hook from the balsa wood in the shape shown left. Glue the hook firmly under the fuselage, near the nose.

When you are sure that all the glue is dry, you can try out your glider. Do this outside where there is plenty of space.

Test flight
To launch the glider, tie the rubber band around the launcher and loop the other end over the hook under the fuselage. Carefully stretch the rubber band, then let the glider go. Always launch your glider outside and away from other people.

Flight control
Your glider should fly in a smooth curve. If it goes into a dive, remove some of the modeling clay from the glider's nose.

Gliders were an important step in the development of powered airplanes. The English inventor, Sir George Cayley, was the first person to build and test gliders. In the early 1850s, he made the first glider to carry a person.

If you were to look at the wings of an airplane, you would find that the top surface of the wing is curved, while the bottom surface is more flat. Most wings have this shape, called an airfoil. Air moves around the airfoil as the airplane flies. This provides the lift that keeps the airplane in the air.

MAKE it WORK!

Using a fan to make air flow past an airfoil, you can investigate the force that keeps an airplane in the air. How does the airfoil perform when it is set at different angles? To be safe, use a fan with a cage or rubber blades, like the one shown here.

1 Cut a rectangle of poster board measuring 4 in. x 12 in. Draw a line across the board, $2/3$ in. from one of the short edges.

2 Fold the poster board in half so that the opposite short edge touches the line. Glue $1/3$ in. of the edge down. You should have a shape with a curved top, as shown right. This is an airfoil.

3 Ask an adult to help make two holes through the center of the airfoil's thickest part, one directly above the other.

You will need
a protractor
cotton thread
a drill or an awl
a wooden block
a desk fan
poster board
stiff wire
scissors
a bead
glue
tape

4 Push the bead onto one end of the wire, bending the wire to hold the bead in place. Push the other end of the wire through the holes in the airfoil.

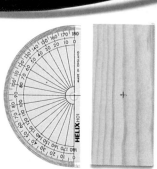

5 With an adult, make a hole in the middle of the wooden block, just big enough to hold the end of the wire. Push the wire into the block so that it stands firmly. You should be able to change the angle of the wire.

6 Attach the protractor to one side of the block, as shown below, using tape.

7 To help you see how air moves over the wing, attach pieces of cotton thread to the airfoil, as shown. The threads will follow the flow of air.

The protractor measures the angle of the airfoil to the airflow.

lift forces the airfoil upward along the length of the wire

flexible flap

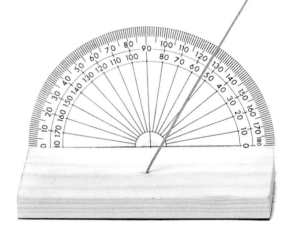

Flying the airfoil

Stand the fan in front of the airfoil, making sure that the rounded edge is facing the fan. This edge is the leading edge, and the other is the trailing edge. The curve of the airfoil means that air moving over the wing travels faster than air moving below the wing.

Fast-moving air does not press against objects as much as slow-moving air. Therefore there is less pressure on the top of the wing than there is on the underside. The higher pressure on the underside pushes up and lifts the wing. The amount of lift generated by the pressure depends on the angle of the wing to the airflow.

*Over 200 years ago Daniel Bernoulli was the first person to realize that air exerts less **pressure** the faster it moves. Today this fact is known as the Bernoulli effect.*

When the airfoil is turned upside down, the air forces it to the ground. To produce an upward force, the curved side of the wing must be on top.

The airfoil creates good lift with its flat edge at a small angle to the stream of air. It is pushed partway up the wire.

The size of the lift force increases with the angle of the airfoil to the wind. Here the airfoil travels quickly to the end of the wire and stays there.

Most early airplanes were triplanes (three sets of wings), or biplanes (two sets). Several short sets of wings gave the airplanes the lift they needed to fly. A monoplane, with just one set of wings, needs longer wings to produce the same amount of lift, but creates less drag than biplanes or triplanes. Most modern airplanes are monoplanes.

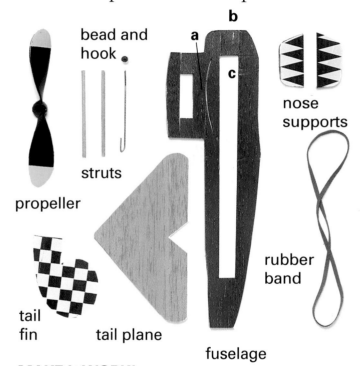

bead and hook

b

a

c

struts

propeller

nose supports

rubber band

tail fin

tail plane

fuselage

MAKE it WORK!
You can make a triplane using balsa wood. You will need to use **struts** to keep the wings rigid.

You will need
glue
a cork
a stapler
stiff wire
a hand drill
a paper clip
a small bead
model propeller
thin balsa wood
a long rubber band

undercarriage

a craft knife
a thick needle
a thin wooden dowel

1 Cut the wing pieces from the balsa wood, as shown below. Make two small holes, one in each end of the middle wing, for the struts.

2 Cut balsa wood shapes for the fuselage (9 in. long, with a slit for the middle wing at **a**), tail fin, and tail plane. Decorate.

3 Glue the tail plane and tail fin to the back of the fuselage, as shown right.

4 Use a thick needle to make a hole in the nose of the fuselage, from **b** to **c**, as shown left. This is the propeller shaft. Cut out two identical nose supports and glue to either side of the fuselage for extra strength. Allow the glue to dry.

5 Straighten out the paper clip and bend one end to form a hook. Push the straight end through the propeller shaft so that the hooked end points backward, toward the tail plane.

6 Push the bead and then the propeller over the wire poking out of the front of the nose. Bend the end of the wire over to hold the bead and propeller in place. The bead forms a bearing that allows the propeller to spin around freely.

three sets of wings
(13-, 12-, 11-in.-long pieces)

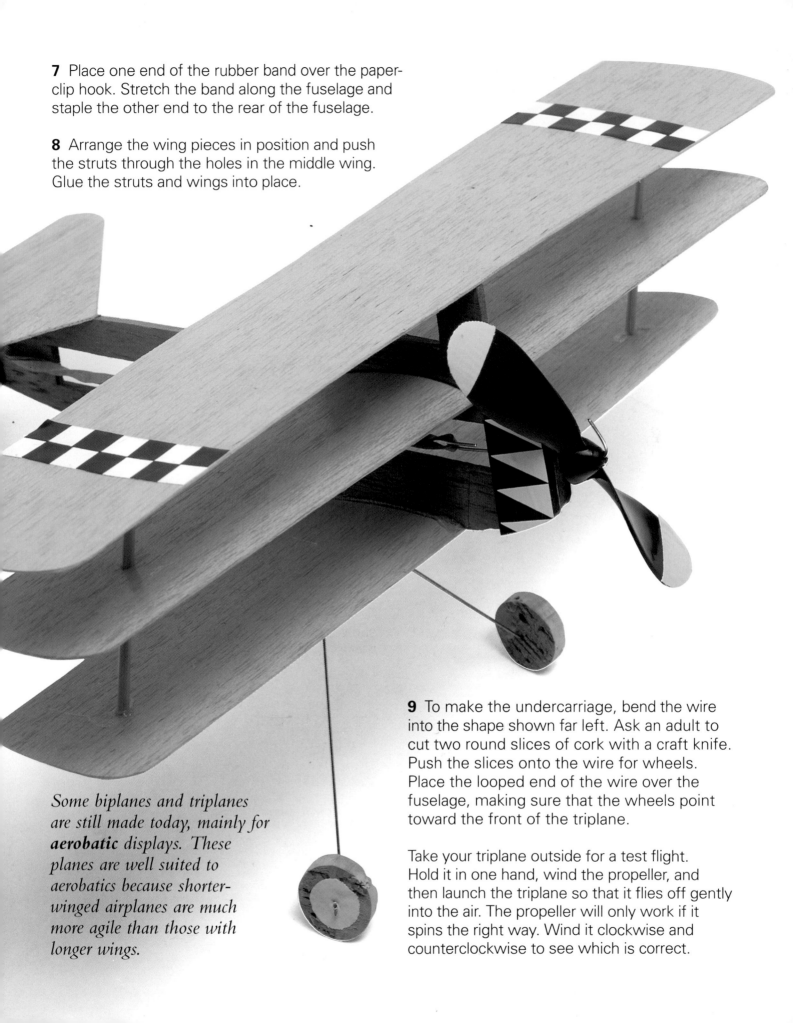

7 Place one end of the rubber band over the paper-clip hook. Stretch the band along the fuselage and staple the other end to the rear of the fuselage.

8 Arrange the wing pieces in position and push the struts through the holes in the middle wing. Glue the struts and wings into place.

*Some biplanes and triplanes are still made today, mainly for **aerobatic** displays. These planes are well suited to aerobatics because shorter-winged airplanes are much more agile than those with longer wings.*

9 To make the undercarriage, bend the wire into the shape shown far left. Ask an adult to cut two round slices of cork with a craft knife. Push the slices onto the wire for wheels. Place the looped end of the wire over the fuselage, making sure that the wheels point toward the front of the triplane.

Take your triplane outside for a test flight. Hold it in one hand, wind the propeller, and then launch the triplane so that it flies off gently into the air. The propeller will only work if it spins the right way. Wind it clockwise and counterclockwise to see which is correct.

28 Delta Wings

Supersonic airplanes travel faster than the speed of sound. They look different from other modern aircraft, often having triangular wings called delta wings. Aircraft with delta wings perform very well at high speeds. Delta wings help to reduce the **sonic boom** that is heard on the ground as an airplane travels faster than sound.

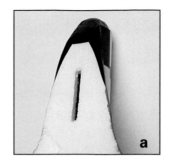
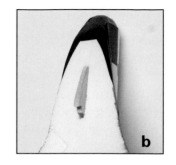

You will need

glue	a wooden dowel
sandpaper	a ping-pong ball
balsa wood	a polystyrene tile
a craft knife	a large rubber band
masking tape	three cardboard tubes
poster board	(4½ in. long)

1 Tape the cardboard tubes together, end to end, to form the fuselage of your shuttle. Glue the ball inside one end of the fuselage so that one half of it is visible.

2 Copy the delta wing shape onto the polystyrene tile–the wings should be the same length as the shuttle fuselage. Ask an adult to help you cut it out. Smooth the edges of the wings with sandpaper.

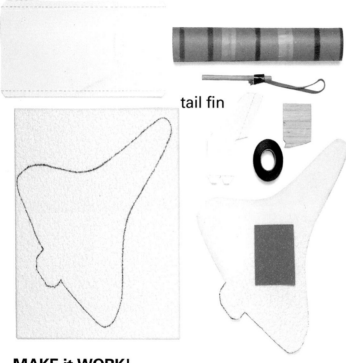

tail fin

MAKE it WORK!

The space shuttle is a reusable aircraft built by **NASA**. It is well suited to traveling fast through the earth's atmosphere because it has delta wings. You can make your own model of the shuttle.

launcher

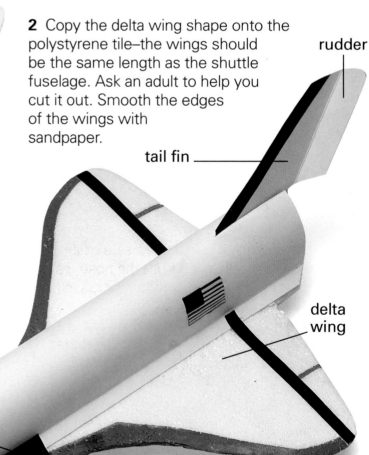

rudder

tail fin

delta wing

fuselage

3 Cut out the tail fin shape from poster board, as shown left. Score and fold along the dotted lines on the base of the fin and the rudder.

4 Cut a rectangle of poster board the same length as the fuselage and wide enough to wrap two-thirds of the way around it. Score along the dotted lines, as shown left, then glue the poster board over the fuselage.

5 Make a 1½-in. slit through the fuselage and poster board at the tail end of the plane. Slip the tail fin gently into it. Glue the flaps at the base of the tail fin inside the cardboard tube fuselage.

6 Place the fuselage in the center of the wings. Tape the poster board flaps of the fuselage to the wings on both sides.

7 Cut out the shape of the launching hook from balsa wood, as shown left.

8 Carefully cut a slit in the underside of the fuselage, a short distance from the nose, as shown in **a**, above left. Glue the hook as in **b**.

9 Cut a length of wooden dowel and tie the rubber band to one end to form the launcher, as shown above. Decorate your model with tape so that it looks like a space shuttle.

The space shuttle weighs 97.5 tons, is 121 ft. long (its fuel tank is 154 ft.), and must travel at 7 mi./second to get into orbit. It is designed for at least 100 space flights.

Test flight

Use the launcher to fly your space shuttle. Loop the rubber band over the hook under the nose. Hold the launcher in one hand and the shuttle firmly in the other. Stretch the rubber band and tilt the shuttle upward slightly, then release it. Always launch your shuttle outside and away from other people. For an alternative shuttle launch, see pages 44-45.

The first space shuttle was launched on April 12, 1981, from Cape Canaveral, Florida.

Airplanes with triangular, swept-back wings, or delta wings, are well suited to high-speed flight. But at low speeds they do not produce as much lift as a plane with ordinary wings. A swing-wing airplane has wings that change during flight between delta wings and ordinary wings, according to its speed.

2 Make the fuselage sides by cutting out two identical poster board shapes, as shown. Score and fold along the dotted lines. Punch a hole in each side, as shown.

3 Cut out two identical wing shapes and punch a hole in each, as shown. Decorate the wing tips with strips of colored tape.

4 Attach the wings to the fuselage by pushing the fasteners through both holes and folding the ends out flat underneath.

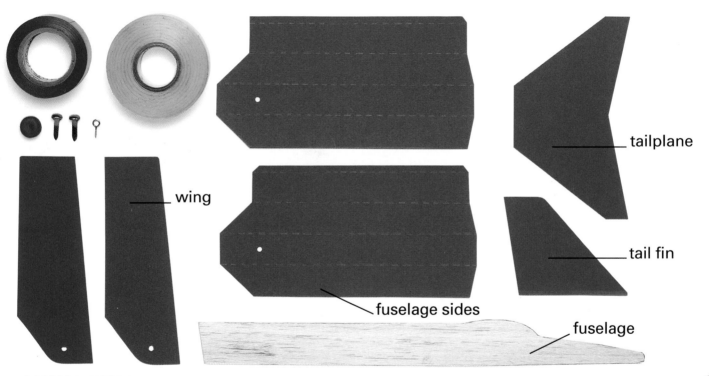

tailplane

wing

tail fin

fuselage sides

fuselage

MAKE it WORK!

If you make a swing-wing glider, you can swing the wings of the glider between two positions and find out how this affects the glider's flight.

You will need

glue	a craft knife
paint	colored tape
modeling clay	a hole punch
balsa wood	two paper fasteners
poster board	the launcher from page 28
a small hook	

1 With an adult cut the fuselage from balsa wood. Paint it and add window shapes cut from tape.

5 Fold the fuselage sides into a long box. Hold each box together by gluing the narrow flap inside. When the glue is dry attach them to either side of the balsa-wood fuselage, also using glue. The angled end should face toward the nose.

6 Cut out the tailplane and tail fin and decorate them with colored tape. Score and fold a narrow flap at the bottom of the tail fin. Glue the flap to the rear of the fuselage and fold the tail fin so that it stands up straight.

7 Cut the tailplane in half to make two smaller wings. Glue each half to the top of the fuselage, at the base of the tail fin.

8 Screw the hook into the underside of the glider, about halfway along the nose.

9 Support the model glider with your finger just under the wings. In order to fly properly, your model must be perfectly balanced. To do this, add or remove small pieces of clay to the nose.

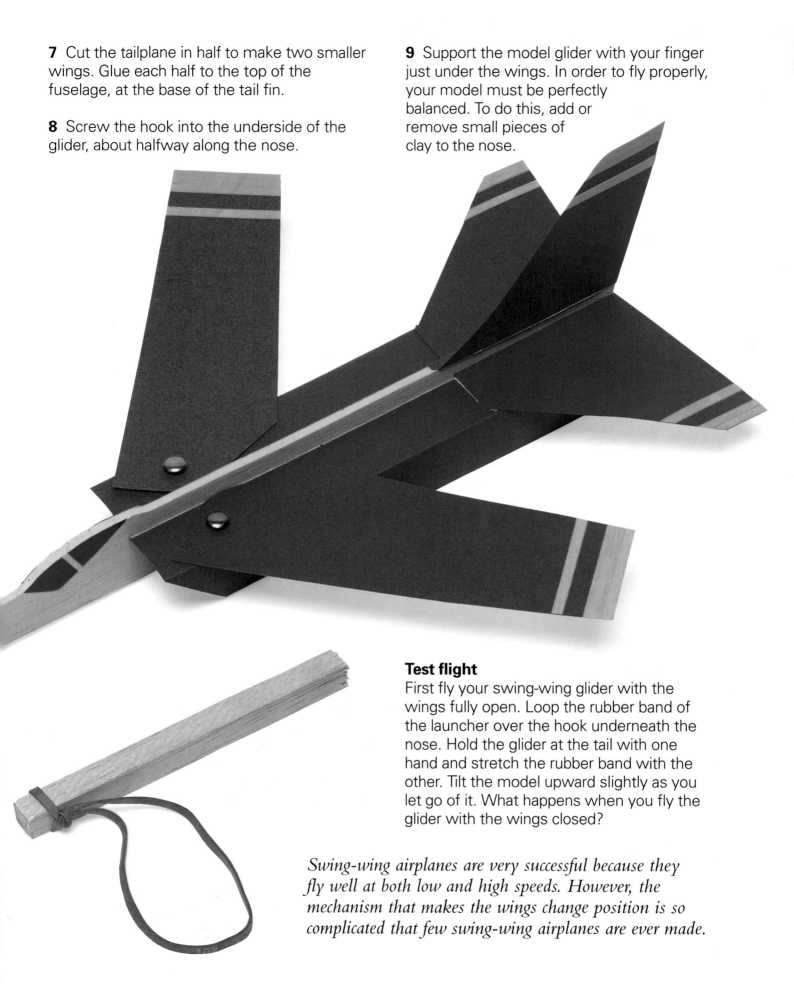

Test flight
First fly your swing-wing glider with the wings fully open. Loop the rubber band of the launcher over the hook underneath the nose. Hold the glider at the tail with one hand and stretch the rubber band with the other. Tilt the model upward slightly as you let go of it. What happens when you fly the glider with the wings closed?

Swing-wing airplanes are very successful because they fly well at both low and high speeds. However, the mechanism that makes the wings change position is so complicated that few swing-wing airplanes are ever made.

An airplane propeller provides thrust in two ways. It has curved blades that disturb the air as they rotate. This creates high-pressure air behind the propeller, which pushes the propeller and the airplane forward. At the same time, the spinning propeller pushes air backward. This also pushes the plane forward. A propeller needs a source of power, usually an engine.

Propellers are curved like an airplane's wing. They produce a force in the same way that a wing produces lift, but this push is directed forward, rather than upward.

MAKE it WORK!

By making a model propeller, you will see how the air is pushed backward as it turns. Your propeller does not need an engine. You will provide the energy to keep it turning.

You will need

modeling clay	a cork
two thin straws	glue
poster board	string
thick balsa wood	ribbons
a thin wooden dowel	hand drill
a thick wooden dowel	a craft knife

1 Ask an adult to cut two rectangles, ³/₄ in. x 2 in., from the balsa wood, with a craft knife.

2 Now ask the adult to drill a hole in the center of each piece, large enough for the thick wooden dowel to pass through.

3 Cut two more blocks, ³/₄ in. x 4 in., from the wood. Glue the 4 blocks together, with the holes facing each other, to form a frame, as shown below.

4 Ask an adult to drill a hole going side to side through one end of the cork.

5 Now make a second hole in the other end of the cork, going from the bottom halfway up into the middle.

6 Push a 12-in. length of thin dowel through the hole going across the top of the cork. Push the end of a 6-in. length of thick dowel up into the hole in the center of the cork.

7 For the propeller blades, first cut four rectangles, 5 in. x 2 in., from poster board.

8 Draw a line down the center of two of the rectangles and glue a straw along each line. Glue the other rectangles on top.

9 Slide the straws onto the thin doweling and secure the ends with modeling clay. Position the blades so that they are at angles to each other.

10 Push the long end of the thick dowel through both holes in the wooden frame.

To see your propeller at work, hold the frame in one hand and twist the thick dowel with the other. Suspend ribbons on a string and point your propeller at them. Which way do you turn the dowel in order to make the ribbons flutter? What happens to the ribbons when you turn the propeller in the other direction?

In 1979, a propeller-driven airplane, the Gossamer Albatross, flew 22 miles between England and France. This plane was unusual because it had pedals and a chain, like those on a bicycle, to transmit power to the propeller.

An airplane with a propeller needs a source of power to make the propeller turn. People have used pedals and even electric motors driven by solar power to turn propellers. Today, most aircraft have propellers driven by internal combustion engines, which are very powerful, yet light. These engines produce power by burning **fuel**.

You will need

a cork	a stapler
stiff wire	modeling clay
strong glue	balsa wood
a paper clip	a craft knife
a model propeller	a small bead
a long rubber band	duct tape
an awl	

1 Ask an adult to help you cut out a 3/8 in. x 10 in. strip of balsa wood for the fuselage. Then cut a 1-in.-wide rectangle for the nose.

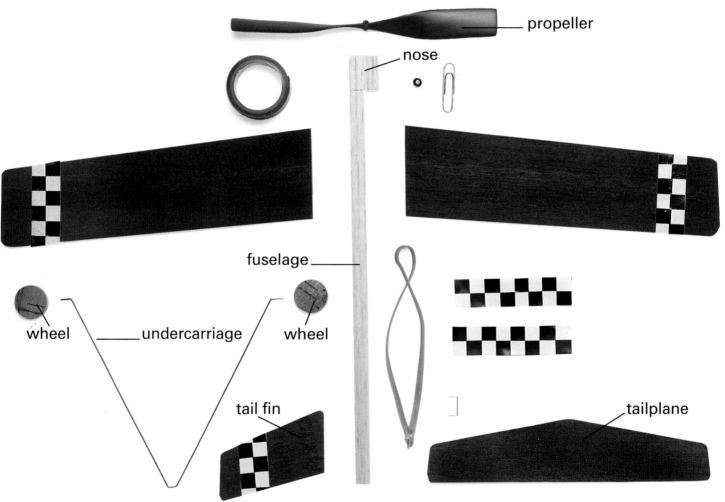

propeller

nose

fuselage

wheel — undercarriage — wheel

tail fin

tailplane

MAKE it WORK!

A rubber band drives the propeller on this model plane. Twisting the rubber band stores energy in it. When the model is released, this energy untwists the rubber band and turns the propeller. The tighter you twist the rubber band, the faster the propeller turns.

2 Glue the nose to one end of the fuselage, then wrap duct tape around it. Make a small hole through the front of the nose, beneath the fuselage, with the awl.

3 Staple the rubber band to the underside of the fuselage, about 2 in. from the tail end.

4 Straighten out the paper clip and push it through the hole in the nose. Slide the bead and the propeller onto the paper clip. Bend the end of the paperclip to hold them in place. Bend the other end of the paper clip on the underside of the fuselage and hook the rubber band over it.

5 Ask an adult to make two 1$2/3$-in. slits in the tail end of the fuselage with a craft knife. Make one slit along the top and the other through the side of the tail, as shown below.

6 Cut a 2 in. x 2$3/4$ in. tail fin from the balsa wood and a 7 in. x 1$2/3$ in. tailplane. Fit both pieces into the fuselage, as shown below.

7 Cut two 8 in. x 2$1/3$ in. wings as shown and glue them to the top of the fuselage so that they are slightly angled upward. Bend the wire into the shape of the undercarriage. Ask an adult to cut two slices off the cork and stick them onto the end of the wire to make the wheels. Now position the undercarriage over the fuselage, as shown.

To fly your plane, hold it gently behind the wings and wind up the propeller. Push the model into the air and release the propeller.

The first successful propelled flight of an airplane was in 1871. The propeller was powered by a wound-up rubber band, and the airplane was only 20 in. long.

Flight control
If your airplane is not stable, wind the propeller in the other direction. The plane should fly in a gentle curve. If it dives, add some modeling clay to the tail. If it stalls, or loses lift, add a little to the nose.

A pilot controls an aircraft in flight using levers and pedals in the cockpit to move the **control surfaces**. Most planes have three types of control surface – ailerons, elevators, and the rudder – that allow the pilot to change direction in the air.

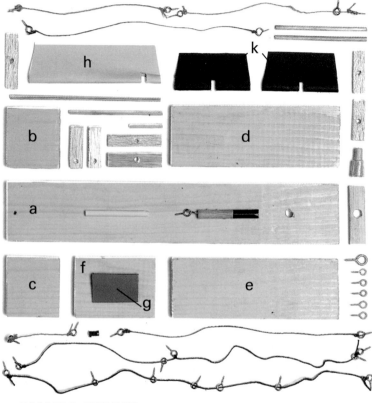

MAKE it WORK!

You can see how a pilot's controls work by making the model cockpit on the next few pages. Use the model glider on page 22 to see how the rudder can control flight.

You will need

saw	strong glue
a hand drill	a craft knife
a long tack	a large hook
balsa wood	thin cardboard
drinking straws	a large eyelet hook
string (red, green)	a thick and thin dowel
small eyelet hooks	three rubber stoppers
plastic tubing to fit thick dowel	
a plank of wood, 3/8 in. thick x 3 in. wide	

The airplane base

1 Ask an adult to saw the plank into six pieces (**a** to **f**) to make the base shown below. The fuselage (**a**) is 10 in. long.

2 Drill a large hole in one end of the fuselage for the thick dowel (rudder pedal) and a smaller hole in the other end for the thin dowel (rudder).

3 Glue base pieces together (except tail fin) and glue rubber stoppers under the base for support.

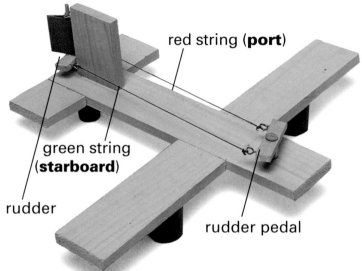

red string (**port**)

green string (**starboard**)

rudder

rudder pedal

The rudder: steering or turning

1 Ask an adult to cut two 3/4 in. x 23/4 in. bars of balsa wood. Drill a large hole in the center of one (the rudder pedal) and a small hole in the center of the other (the rudder). Screw one small eyelet hook into each end of both bars, as shown.

2 To make the rudder pedal, push 11/2 in. of thick dowel into the hole in the fuselage nose. Cover the dowel with 3/4 in. of tubing. Push a long tack through the hole in the pedal and then into the dowel, keeping the eyelets facing the tail.

3 Make a rudder flap by gluing a piece of cardboard 21/3 in. x 3 in. (**g**) around a 3-in. length of straw. To fix the flap to the rudder, cut 5 in. of thin dowel and push it through the straw. Push the dowel through the hole in the rudder, a 3/4-in. length of straw, and, lastly, through the hole in the fuselage tail.

4 Screw a large eyelet hook into the back of the tail fin. Glue the tail fin into place, sliding the hook over the thin dowel holding the rudder flap. When the glue is dry, tie red and green string between the eyelets on the rudder and rudder pedal.

The control stick

1 Cut 3½ in. of thick dowel for the control stick. Screw one small eyelet into the bottom of the stick and another 1 in. from the base. Screw a hook into the fuselage, behind the rudder pedal. Slide the eyelet over the hook in the fuselage.

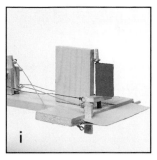

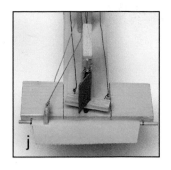

The elevator

1 Cut a balsa wood bar, 2¾ in. x ¾ in., and drill a small hole through the center. Screw an eyelet into each end, on the same side, as **i** above.

2 Cut an 8 in. x 6 in. piece of cardboard and fold it in half. Glue a straw along the inside fold. Cut a 1-in. slit near one end, as shown left in **h**.

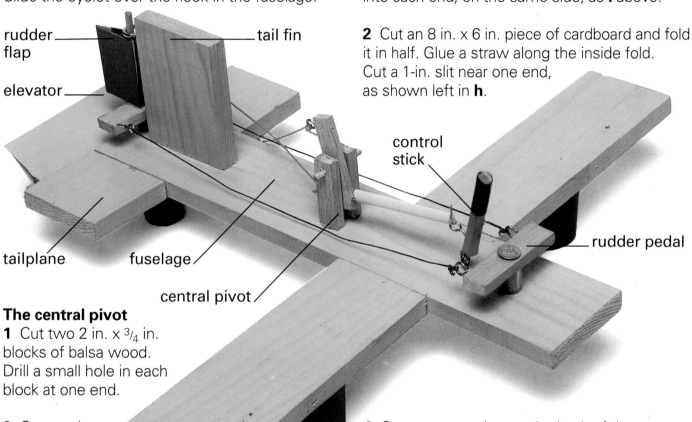

rudder flap — tail fin

elevator —

tailplane — fuselage —

control stick

rudder pedal

central pivot —

wing

The central pivot

1 Cut two 2 in. x ¾ in. blocks of balsa wood. Drill a small hole in each block at one end.

2 Cut another 2¾ in. x ¾ in. block and drill a small hole through the center. Screw an eyelet into each end on opposite sides as above. Tie a 10 in. piece of string to each eyelet.

3 Position the larger block between the smaller ones, as above, so that the holes line up. Glue the outer blocks to the fuselage. When dry, slip in the middle block and push a length of thin dowel through all three holes.

3 Screw two eyelets to the back of the tailplane, 8 in. apart. Slip the bar vertically into the slit on the cardboard flap. Slide 8½-in. thin dowel through the eyelets, elevator flap, and bar, as in **j** above.

4 Tie a string from the top of the central pivot to the bottom of the bar and another from the bottom of the pivot to the top of the bar. Then thread a 3-in. string through a piece of straw. Tie one end to the eyelet in the control stick and the other to the eyelet at the base of the pivot.

Now move the control stick and rudder pedal to see the effect on the elevator and rudder.

Airplanes have movable flaps called ailerons at the trailing edge of each wing. They are designed so that when one is up, the other is down. Ailerons are used with the rudder in a turning maneuver called **banking**.

MAKE it WORK!

By using the rudder pedal and control stick on pages 36-37, you can see how an airplane can turn, climb, and dive. Now add ailerons to learn how more advanced maneuvers, such as **yaw**, banking, or rolling are carried out.

The ailerons: rolling or banking

Make the ailerons in the same way that you made the elevator and rudder (pages 36-37).

1 Cut two pieces of balsa wood 2¾ in. x ¾ in. Drill a hole in the center of both bars, wide enough for a thin dowel to pass through.

2 Cut two poster board rectangles, 5½ in. x 4 in. Fold them in half and glue a straw along the fold (see **k**, page 36). Glue the flaps around the straw.

3 Cut a notch ⅜ in. deep in the center of each folded poster board (through the straw).

4 Screw two small hooks into the ends of each balsa-wood bar. Then screw two hooks into the trailing edge of each wing, 4 in. apart.

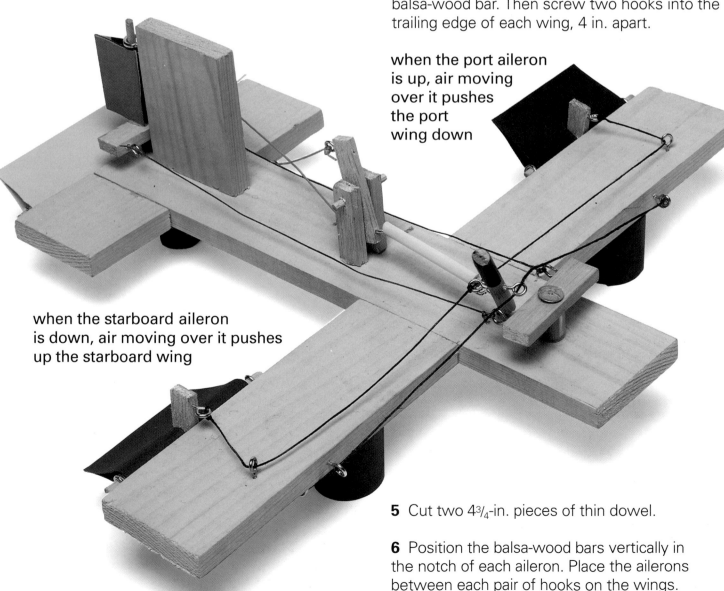

when the port aileron is up, air moving over it pushes the port wing down

when the starboard aileron is down, air moving over it pushes up the starboard wing

5 Cut two 4¾-in. pieces of thin dowel.

6 Position the balsa-wood bars vertically in the notch of each aileron. Place the ailerons between each pair of hooks on the wings.

 left turn

right turn

Left and right turning or banking

By adding ailerons to the glider you made on page 22, you can make it turn to the left and right, as above. Use blue cardboard for making the ailerons, as below.

When the starboard aileron is up and the port aileron is down, the airplane rolls to the right. When the rudder is moved to the right at the same time, the airplane turns smoothly to the right. Reverse the positions to make a left turn.

Early airplanes did not have ailerons. Pilots changed direction in midair by pulling levers that made the whole wing change shape.

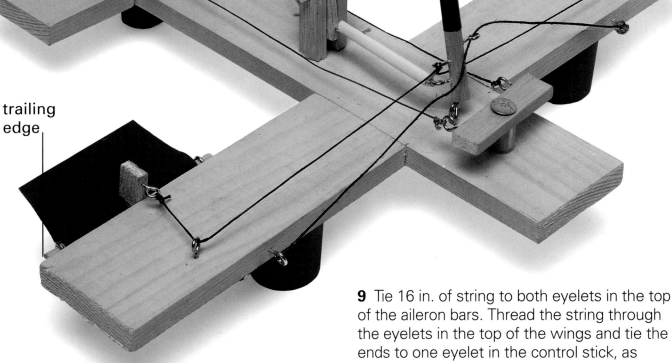

trailing edge

7 Slide the dowel through the hooks, aileron, and balsa wood to hold in place.

8 Screw three small eyelets into each wing: one on top; the second under the wing, directly below the first; and the third in the center of the front edge of the wing. Screw two more hooks onto either side of the control stick.

9 Tie 16 in. of string to both eyelets in the top of the aileron bars. Thread the string through the eyelets in the top of the wings and tie the ends to one eyelet in the control stick, as shown above. The string should be taut.

10 Repeat step 9, but thread the string from the bottom of the aileron bar, underneath the wings, to the other eyelet on the control stick.

Moving the control stick to the left and right pulls the strings and raises and lowers the two ailerons. When one is up, the other is down.

The rotor of a helicopter acts like a cross between an airplane wing and a propeller. It provides both lift to keep the helicopter in the air and thrust to push it forward. The helicopter can take off and land vertically, move in any direction, or remain hanging in one place in the air.

3 Draw a circle, with a diameter of 3/4 in., in the center. Cut along the solid lines to the circle and then score and fold along the dotted lines. Glue a circle of different colored poster board inside the central circle on the top of your rotor.

4 Use an awl to make a small hole in the middle of a cork. Push a 5-in. length of dowel into the hole. Stick the rotor of your spinner onto the cork. Wind the string around the dowel and then push the dowel through the thread spool as shown below.

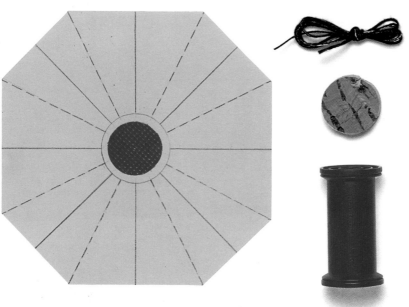

Holding the spool in one hand and the string in the other, pull the string and launch your spinner. If it fails, try winding the string the other way.

The design of the helicopter was based on a toy from China in the 1500's.

MAKE it WORK!
You can make two models to look at the way a helicopter rotor works. Both will take off if you spin them fast enough.

To make a rotor you will need

a cork	glue
an awl	string
poster board	a protractor
a thin wooden dowel	an empty thread spool

1 Cut poster board into a 4-in. square. Draw two solid lines through the center and two across the diagonal, as shown. Trim the corners.

2 Line up the center of the protractor with the center of the square and draw dotted lines at 20° to each side of the diagonal lines.

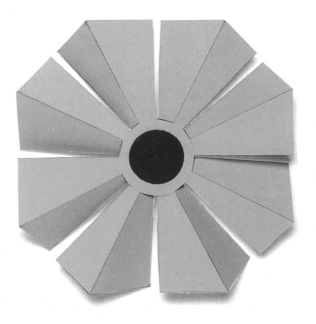

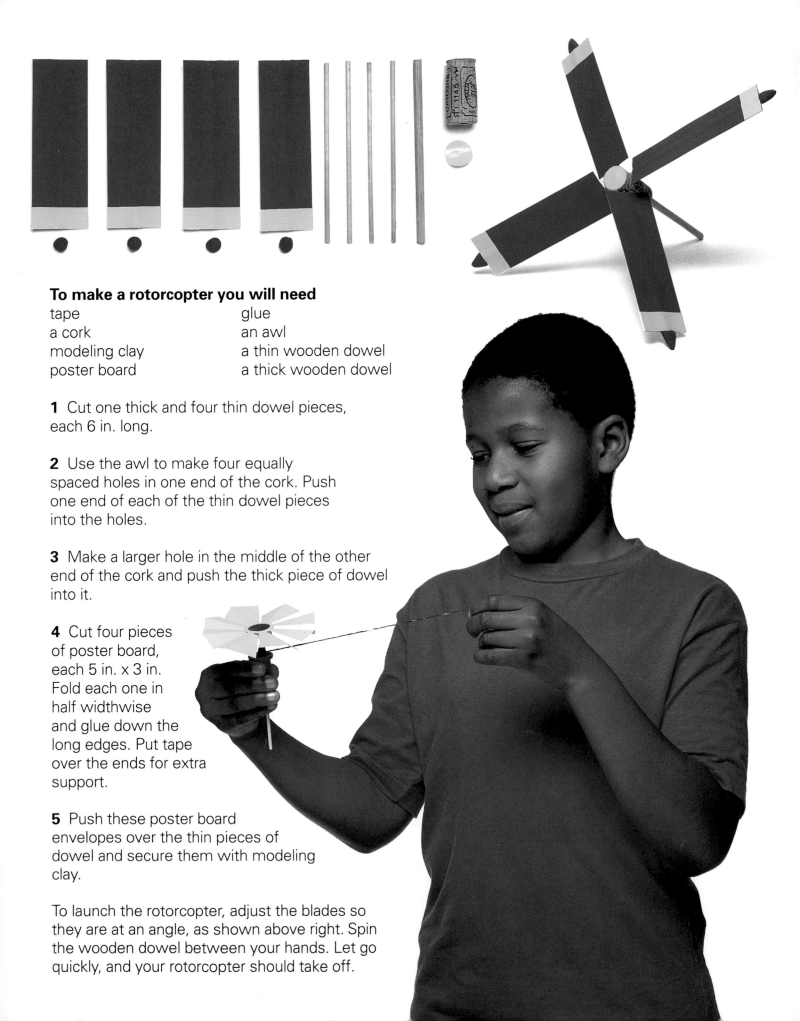

To make a rotorcopter you will need

tape
a cork
modeling clay
poster board

glue
an awl
a thin wooden dowel
a thick wooden dowel

1 Cut one thick and four thin dowel pieces, each 6 in. long.

2 Use the awl to make four equally spaced holes in one end of the cork. Push one end of each of the thin dowel pieces into the holes.

3 Make a larger hole in the middle of the other end of the cork and push the thick piece of dowel into it.

4 Cut four pieces of poster board, each 5 in. x 3 in. Fold each one in half widthwise and glue down the long edges. Put tape over the ends for extra support.

5 Push these poster board envelopes over the thin pieces of dowel and secure them with modeling clay.

To launch the rotorcopter, adjust the blades so they are at an angle, as shown above right. Spin the wooden dowel between your hands. Let go quickly, and your rotorcopter should take off.

42 Jet Engines

A jet engine is much more powerful than a propeller. It works by burning fuel to heat air that is taken in at the front of the engine. The air expands as it is heated and leaves at high speed from the back of the engine. The escaping gases produce a strong forward thrust, which pushes the aircraft through the air.

For the jet balloons you will need

tape
string
long balloons

balloon pump
drinking straws

1 Thread two straws onto the string. Tie the string to two chairs, placed quite far apart, for your balloon run. The string should be taut.

2 Blow up a balloon with a balloon pump and hold the end to keep the air in. Ask a friend to tape the straws to the balloon.

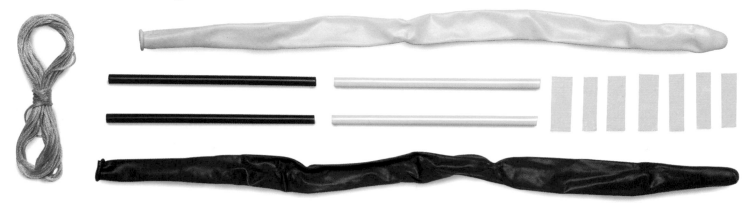

MAKE it WORK!

You can make two models that work in a similar way to a jet engine. The jet balloons allow you to control the thrust produced by high-pressure air escaping from a balloon. You can also make a "**vertical** take-off and landing" (VTOL) aircraft that flies upward when powered by two balloons.

Slide the balloon to one end of the string and let go, so the air can escape. The balloon should whizz along the string to the other end. For more flights, bring the balloon back to the start and blow it up again. The jet balloons work in a similar way to a jet engine. Air thrown out at the back of the balloon pushes the balloon forward at high speed.

The open neck of the balloon allows air to escape. This propels the balloon forward.

You could set up two strings and have a balloon race. Does twice as much air in the balloon make it go twice as far or twice as fast?

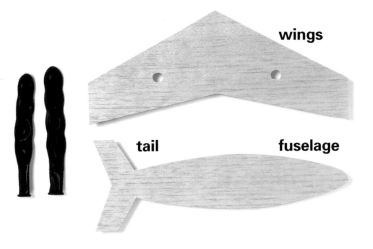

wings

tail   **fuselage**

The jets of air from the balloons push the plane up from the ground. With a real VTOL airplane, air from the engine is directed downward at take-off. The air pushes the plane upward. When the airplane is flying **horizontally**, air is directed backward, giving thrust to push the plane forward.

For the VTOL airplane you will need

glue   paint
a craft knife   thin balsa wood
two new long balloons   balloon pump

1 Draw the fuselage and tail (9 in. long), and the wings (9 in. wide) on the balsa wood as shown above. Ask an adult to help you cut out the pieces.

2 Make a hole in each side of the wings, large enough to push the end of a balloon through (about 3/8 in.).

3 Paint the pieces of your plane. When they are dry, stick the wings onto the middle of the fuselage.

4 Blow up two balloons. Ask a friend to help you push the ends down through each hole without letting the air out. Hold the balloon ends close to the floor, keeping the plane level. Let go of both balloons at the same time and the plane will fly upward.

44 Rockets

Rockets are **projectiles** driven by the forward thrust produced when hot gases are forced out of the back of the rocket's engine. The hot gases are produced as rocket fuel burns. This process needs oxygen. Jet engines can use oxygen from the air, but rockets need to carry their own supply because they travel beyond earth's atmosphere, where there is no air.

You will need

tape	a paper clip
glue	a plastic bottle
scissors	thick cardboard
an awl	poster board
carpet tape	a small air valve
a bicycle pump	a rubber stopper
	two kitchen roll tubes
	the space shuttle model
	(pages 28 - 29)

MAKE it WORK!

You can make a rocket to launch your space shuttle model from pages 28 - 29. A space shuttle is helped into orbit by two powerful rocket engines that separate from the shuttle at a height of about 30 miles and parachute back to earth.

You can try some experiments with your rocket. Does it fly as high if you fill the bottle with water? What happens if you don't put any water in at all?

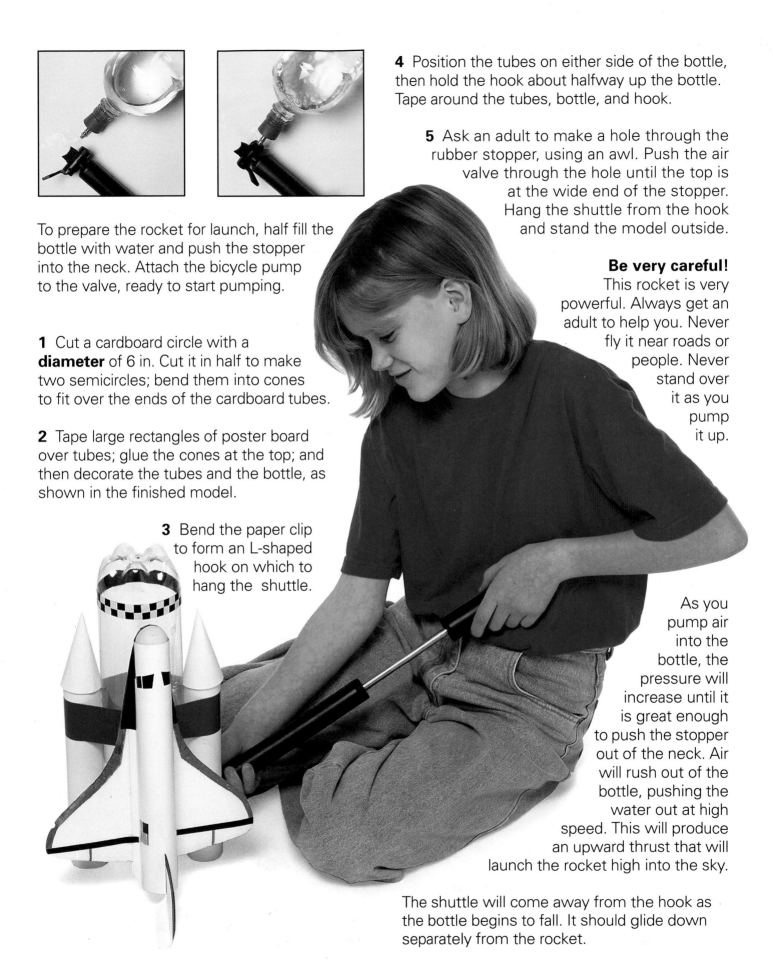

4 Position the tubes on either side of the bottle, then hold the hook about halfway up the bottle. Tape around the tubes, bottle, and hook.

5 Ask an adult to make a hole through the rubber stopper, using an awl. Push the air valve through the hole until the top is at the wide end of the stopper. Hang the shuttle from the hook and stand the model outside.

Be very careful!
This rocket is very powerful. Always get an adult to help you. Never fly it near roads or people. Never stand over it as you pump it up.

To prepare the rocket for launch, half fill the bottle with water and push the stopper into the neck. Attach the bicycle pump to the valve, ready to start pumping.

1 Cut a cardboard circle with a **diameter** of 6 in. Cut it in half to make two semicircles; bend them into cones to fit over the ends of the cardboard tubes.

2 Tape large rectangles of poster board over tubes; glue the cones at the top; and then decorate the tubes and the bottle, as shown in the finished model.

3 Bend the paper clip to form an L-shaped hook on which to hang the shuttle.

As you pump air into the bottle, the pressure will increase until it is great enough to push the stopper out of the neck. Air will rush out of the bottle, pushing the water out at high speed. This will produce an upward thrust that will launch the rocket high into the sky.

The shuttle will come away from the hook as the bottle begins to fall. It should glide down separately from the rocket.

Aerobatics Spectacular stunts performed in the air. The pilots in aerobatic displays make their airplanes twist and turn and do tricks.

Air resistance A force that slows down any object moving through the air. The faster an object moves, the greater the air resistance.

Atmosphere The blanket of air around the earth. The atmosphere is a mixture of gases. We breathe the lower atmosphere, called the troposphere, which consists of nitrogen (78%), oxygen (21%), and small amounts of argon, water vapor, and carbon dioxide.

Banking The way in which an airplane turns to the left or right in the air. During banking, the pilot uses the ailerons to roll the airplane a little and then uses the rudder to take the airplane into a smooth turn.

Control surfaces The parts of an airplane that are used to control the aircraft during flight and to help the pilot change direction. There are three main types of control surfaces: ailerons, elevators, and rudders.

Density The mass of an object divided by its volume. Polystyrene has a lower density than steel: a block of polystyrene would weigh less than a block of steel of the same size.

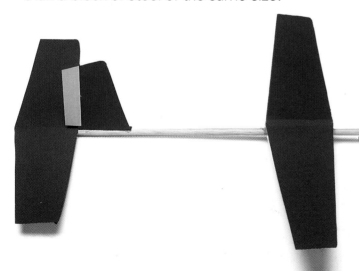

Diameter The distance measured across a circle, passing through the center.

Drag The air resistance acting on airplanes. Drag acts in the opposite direction of thrust.

Energy When something has energy, it has the ability to make other things move and change. People use energy stored in their muscles to push and pull loads. Aircraft engines use the energy stored in fuel to provide the thrust needed for flight.

Force A push or pull that is used to lift something, start it moving, or hold it in place against another force, such as gravity. Objects do not have to touch to exert forces on each other. Four forces act on an airplane. They are gravity, lift, drag, and thrust.

Fuel A substance, such as gasoline, burned to produce heat and used to make engines work.

Gravity The force that makes objects fall toward the earth. It is because of gravity that things feel heavy. For an object to fly, an upward force must act upon it to overcome the pull of gravity.

Horizontal Parallel to, or in line with, the horizon. Horizontal is the opposite of vertical.

Lift A force that acts upward against gravity and makes it possible for airplanes, airships, and balloons to rise in the air.

Mass The amount of matter in a substance. The more mass an object has, the more it weighs.

NASA The abbreviation for the National Aeronautics and Space Administration.

Phenakistoscope A spinning disk used to show moving pictures. A series of images on the disk, when viewed one after the other, gives the illusion of movement.

Port The left side of an airplane, as seen by the pilot facing the airplane's nose.

Power The rate at which something uses energy. An engine with high power uses energy more quickly than a less powerful one and produces a great deal of thrust.

Pressure The pushing force on a surface.

Projectile An object, such as a cannonball or a rocket, that is thrown forward and launched into the air.

Radius The distance measured from the center of a circle to its edge.

Rotate To move around a central point. A propeller rotates around its central hub.

Sonic boom A loud, explosive sound, like a thunderclap, that is caused by the shockwaves an aircraft creates when traveling faster than the speed of sound.

Stability A measure of how hard it is to knock an object off balance.

Starboard The right-hand side of an airplane, as seen by the pilot facing the nose of the aircraft.

Strain A measure of the force needed to stretch an object.

Strut A solid bar placed between the wings of a biplane to hold them rigid.

Supersonic A supersonic airplane, such as Concorde, that is capable of traveling faster than the speed of sound.

Thrust A force that pushes an airplane forward through the air.

Trajectory The curved path that a projectile follows as it travels through the air.

Vertical Perpendicular, or at right angles to, the horizon. Vertical is the opposite of horizontal.

Yaw The way an airplane twists to the left and to the right when in flight.